TORMENTED SOULS

LENITA J WASHINGTON

ISBN: 979-8-9856253-0-1

Dedication

I dedicate this book to my late father, who passed away from cancer in May 2013 and is now with his Father up in Heaven. I want to give honor to God first and foremost for blessing me with a father that gave his best by raising me and my sisters and did an awesome job doing it. I thank you, Daddy, for giving me the strength and the ability to grow into the woman that I am today. I also thank you for inspiring me to write this book; it was you in my dreams talking to me, and now I get it. I love you with all my heart. "I did it"

Love You!

Contents

Chapter 1

The Family Tree

As a child, I always thought that a mother should be willing to raise her children the best way she can by any means necessary. That means not abusing them in any way, and if you must get two or even three jobs to put food on the table and clothes on their backs, then so be it. Well . . . I had been wrong about my mother. She didn't give a shit about nothing or nobody. It was all about her and her selfish ways.

I remembered every day of the week was a beautiful day. The sun was always shining, birds were always chirping, and the sky was always blue. We lived out in Willow Groove in the countryside in a quiet neighborhood. I had two sisters—Stacey, who is one year and eight months older than me, and Destiny, who was just a baby at the time—and three brothers. My brothers, Frank, David, and Keon, were all older than me and my sisters. Frank, my sisters, and I were raised together in our mother's household. He didn't share the same dad as us, just the same mom. His father had passed away a long time ago, before we were born. Well . . . at least, that's what we were told. Our Big Mom—that's my mother's mom—was one mean grandmom. She would babysit us when Mother ran the streets. David and Keon lived with their mother, however; we shared the same dad. My mom and dad were a hot mess, having all these kids. My goodness!

My dad was a Philadelphia police officer. He worked at Precinct 17 for many years. My mother had a variety of jobs but didn't really stay at one job long enough for me to remember. We didn't see Dad as much, because they weren't together and were never married. Every now and then, though, Dad would stop by to pay us a visit and give Mother some money to take care of us, which she still never took time out to do.

Mother would have us moving from place to place. One minute we were in a nice big, beautiful house, and then the next minute we were living out of bags staying in a nasty small hotel room. She wasn't stable at all. We didn't understand why we were always struggling, not to mention homeless. Despite it all, we always remained happy.

Lenita J Washington

Chapter 2

The Crazy Lady

Two years had gone by, and we finally moved into a nice big house in an all-white neighborhood in the suburbs. Stacey, some neighborhood kids, and I were playing upstairs in our room while Destiny was asleep in her crib.

My brother Frank, Mother, and their friends were downstairs in the living room smoking weed and drinking liquor. They wouldn't let us play downstairs while they were entertaining their company, so we would run to the top of the steps and scream downstairs to scare them, then run away laughing. My mom would yell at the top of the stairs, "Get y'all fucking asses away from the steps and get in the bed!"

Just as I was about to run away from the steps, a white woman came busting through the front door screaming. So, I stood at the top of the steps for a second to be noisy again, but everybody downstairs had started screaming and running around the house in circles when the lady came busting through the front door. See, they were all downstairs getting high, so the weed had them looking crazy and acting stupid.

While everyone was running all over the place, the lady made her way up to the steps and screamed, "He's going to kill me!" She grabbed me and threw me in front of her to shield herself. I thought, *Why in the hell is she using my little ass to protect her? I can't save her.* My mom told the lady to come downstairs and just climb out the window and run. The lady replied, "I can't! He's seen me run in this house and he's going to kill me." My mom said, "Exactly, that's why you need to get your ass out of here before he kills all of us!" The lady then climbed out the window and began to run into the woods.

Shortly after that, the man she was talking about came banging on our door furiously, yelling and demanding that she come out. My brother swung the door open with his high ass, asking the man who he was looking for. He explained he had seen his wife run into this house and she needed to get home right now. My brother told the man he didn't see any women run into the house and slammed the door in his face.

Chapter 3

Taking Care of Ourselves

When Mom was about to run the streets, she would drop us off at Big Mom's house or leave us in the house by ourselves. My brother Frank tried to take care of us at times, but he really couldn't; he was a young kid himself and wanted to hang out with his friends. Dad was always at work or missing in action. There was hardly any food in the house, and my sisters and I stayed hungry.

One time my sisters and I wanted something to eat because we were hungry and hadn't eaten that entire day. So, we used a chair to climb up onto the counter and cracked some eggs in the Crock-Pot and made us some scrambled eggs.

When Big Mom would catch us in the kitchen or doing something she thought we had no business doing, she would take the plastic towel holder stick from the bathroom and whip our little butts with it. We didn't like when Big Mom babysat us; she was mean, and we were afraid of her. Big Mom would whip the shit out of us for any little reason. This time, we didn't care—ass kicking or not, we were hungry and wanted something to eat.

We had to wash our clothes with our feet. Mom would throw clothes in the tub so we could stomp on them. Stacey would stomp one end, and I would stomp the other, then we both would come together and stomped the middle. We would then wring all the clothes out and hang them around the house to dry.

Stacey and I did a lot of things on our own, as young as we were. Our friends were having fun doing kid stuff, while we were in the house cooking, cleaning, babysitting, and washing clothes with our feet.

Going to school was always a problem for me. I think I started the first grade three or four times a year because of moving place to place with my mother. I used to cry when it was time to go to school. I never knew why, but I would just start crying when we had to leave, and Stacey would just look at me and shake her head.

Chapter 4

Visiting Nanny and Grandpop

My sisters and I started spending more time over at our Nanny and Grandpop's house. They were my dad's parents, and my two half-brothers on my dad's side—David and Keon—lived there too. They were our oldest brothers. We all had the same dad but different mothers. Nanny was sweet and funny, and Grandpa stayed in his room watching TV and drinking his liquor most of the time. He was more so like a grumpy old man to me.

Our older brothers would take us to the store, buy us candy, and let us hang out with them when we would come over and visit. They made sure the boys around the way didn't flirt with us, because if they did, they would go beat them up. I was a tough girl; I liked to play ball and race with the boys, and Stacey was tough too. She liked to ride on the front handlebars of David's bike until one day she flipped off.

Stacey had put her foot in the front wheel of the bike and David tried to grab her, but she flipped over and busted her chin on the cement. Stacey was screaming and crying with blood running down her neck while David was panicking, trying to stop the bleeding. Keon came running to Stacey's rescue and was like, "Oh damn, David, you fucked up!" David, pushing Keon, said, "Shut up, man, and help me get her to the house." They rushed Stacey into the house and Dad said, "Whatcha done did now?" Keon replied, "Not me . . . David." Dad rushed into the car and drove our sister to the emergency room. Once we arrived at the hospital, she was seen right away by the doctor and got four stitches under her chin. After Stacey was all stitched up and ready to go, we headed back to Nanny's house to have dinner.

Nanny was the best cook in the whole wide world. That night, she had made some homemade chicken soup for dinner. Her chicken soup was one of my favorite meals she ever made—up until I bit into something hard and white in my bowl. Stacey and Destiny started laughing and teasing me. I told Nanny about it, and she told me to just eat my food. "It's only chicken cartilage!" I'm like, "Chicken cartilage? What the heck is that?" So, I kept complaining about it until finally she yelled, "Ladesa, I put knuckles in the soup. Now eat the damn knuckle soup!" When Nanny said that, I got up from the table, ran into the kitchen, and poured my soup in the sink. Everybody at the table began to laugh at me and I told Nanny to make me cheese sandwich, because you can never go wrong with a cheese sandwich. After dinner, my dad told us to get ready to leave so he could drop us off back with our mother. We were sad that we had to leave as we hugged our brothers, Grandpop, and Nanny goodbye.

Lenita J Washington

Chapter 5

Meet Your Stepmother

A few weeks later, Dad came by to pick me and my sisters up from Mom's and told her that he was taking us to visit Nanny. We were so happy, jumping up and down, dancing in circles, doing all sorts of tricks. We rushed into our room to put some decent clothes on, but there wasn't nothing for us to wear. Either our clothes were dirty or we just had no clothes to wear. Plus, our hair looked a hot mess. However, we were somehow able to find something to wear and put our hair into quick ponytails. Look . . . we were trying to hurry up and get the heck up out of that miserable house.

When we got to Nanny's, our cousin Lamara, who lived right down the street from Nanny's house in West Philly, took us to get all cute and pretty. Stacey, Destiny, and I didn't understand why we were getting our hair done and buying new clothes, but we sure didn't mind it. Once Cousin Lamara had us all polished, Dad came and picked the three of us up. He was amazed and surprised at how beautiful we looked. Shit—hell, we were surprised at how we looked ourselves! There were hardly any days that we looked as gorgeous as we did on that day. Stacey, Destiny, and I finally looked like the little girls that we had always dreamed of being.

We were on our way with Dad, all pretty and dressed up, to go to this special place he had planned for us to go. We arrived at this house with a lady standing in the doorway. She had two cute Pillsbury's chocolate boys standing behind her that were three and four years younger than Stacey and me. I guess you could say everyone was thrilled to see each other. The adults had the surprised, happy, "heard all about you, finally get to meet you" faces, while my sister and I had the "happy to see you, I guess? Who are you? But excited to meet you" type of expression instead. After all the looking each other up and down, we were introduced to one another. The nice lady's name was Glenda, and the two boys standing next to her were her sons, Mark and Stephan.

Ms. Glenda took me and my sisters out to go shopping at the mall and out to eat. She bought us some new clothes, and we finally got our ears pierced! I was like, "Okay, that's a bonus for her. I think I'm liking this lady already." We were enjoying everything Ms. Glenda was doing for us—the types of things we never did while living with our mother. All she wanted to do was get high and run the streets. I guess someone else had to show us what it felt like to have a caring mother and how to have fun as little girls.

After the long day with Ms. Glenda, we went back to her house where Dad and the boys had stayed behind. We all gathered in the living room, Dad popped some popcorn, and we watched some movies on TV. Ms. Glenda looked at my sisters and I with this weird smile on her face while we were watching TV. I looked back at her like, "Okaaay . . . what the fuck are you looking at?" She finally opened her mouth and said, "Do you girls want to call me Ms. Glenda, or Mommy?" We looked at each other with so much joy on our faces and shouted, "Mommy!" Everyone jumped up and started hugging us. That was the happiest day of our lives.

She showed us our new room, which we had to share with Mark and Stephan; we couldn't have our own room because it was only a two-bedroom house. It had two beds in the room and one dresser. Mark and Stephan had to share the bed together, and Stacey, Destiny, and I shared the other one. There were too many of us in that bedroom, but that's how we had to do it that night and many nights after that. My sisters and I didn't care, though, because we finally had clothes, food, and happiness.

Chapter 6

Living With Our New Family

Stacey and I figured that this was our home for good. Destiny was about five years old, so she really didn't care to notice too much of anything. We hadn't heard from or seen our mother anymore after that. It was like we had started to forget about her anyway. We were enrolled in school, had good home-cooked meals, and had a lot of nice clothes to wear now. We also had to do things that kids at our age didn't like to do: chores.

Ms. Glenda had me and my sisters cleaning everything—dishes, bathrooms, scrubbing the floor on our knees, using the toothbrush to get into places that couldn't be reached. Anything you could think of, she had us doing it. Stacey said to me one day, "Why Stephan and Mark don't never have to do any cleaning?" I said, "Because they're fat and greedy, that's why." See, I'm the one with all the mouth, and I didn't care if anybody didn't like it. Stacey is the quiet one; she used to let people walk all over her, and Destiny is shy. She never had anything to say.

Later on, we finally had the opportunity to meet Glenda's family. It was on Christmas Day when her mother, father, sisters, and brothers came over. We had so much fun that day that I would never forget it! My sisters and I had never experienced so much family love. Our favorite step-aunt was Aunt Becky, because she didn't take any mess from anyone, and she was cool. The second favorite aunt was Aunt Wendy; she was pretty, and had beautiful long hair. Our third step-aunt, Aunt Brady, was the rich, sharp, and elegant one. Now the brothers, on the other hand, were handsome-looking and funny. My favorite step-uncle was Uncle Eric. He was cool and mean—in a good way. Ms. Glenda's family took us in as if we were their blood family.

Chapter 7

Moving to a New Neighborhood

L ife became great with our new family, and we were able to move to a bigger and better house in Germantown. It may not have had a lot of rooms, but it was one more room greater than the last one. It was a nice neighborhood with lots of kids that we could play with and a great school system. I was so happy to start school so I could meet my new classmates and teacher. The school I attended was Pastorius Elementary. I ran track, played violin, and attended choir classes. Moving in with Stepmom and going to school was the best thing that could have ever happened to us.

I made two best friends at school, Kendra and Solange. We often hung out in the candy store. Sunflower seeds and Mr G's hot chips were our favorite. Stacey had her own corny girlfriends, and half the time she stayed on the porch reading her novels. Mark and Stephen did their own thing; they stayed up under each other. They had neighborhood friends, but they were also content with just playing with each other. I also stayed fighting my big sister's battles. I didn't like for anyone to mess with my sister.

Stacey was on the front porch one day reading one of her drama books when this bully girl decided she wanted to mess with my sister for no reason. She was mean, big, and could fight her ass off. Everybody feared her, both in school and around the neighborhood. That day, she picked the wrong family to be bullying. This girl, Badrea, started teasing Stacey, calling her a nerd and putting her fingers in her face. Stacey just sat there, reading her book and not saying a word because she feared her. Meanwhile, I was at the corner store being greedy, buying me some sunflower seeds. Badrea came onto the porch and slapped Stacey in the face. Stacey just sat there and didn't do or say anything.

I was on my way home from the store and my neighborhood friends started telling me that Badrea slapped Stacey. I saw Stacey on the porch crying, reading her book. I asked her what was wrong, and she said, "Badrea slapped me in the face." I said, "What?! I'm going to kick her ass!" I stopped eating my sunflower seeds, ran down the street, and confronted her. Stacey must have run into the house to tell my dad, because she already knew what I was going to do. Yep . . . kick-ass time. I asked her, "Why you slap my sister?" She said, "Because I wanted to . . . why?" Before I knew it, my fist was in her face and then we were on the ground, punching and scratching. She was pulling my hair, and I was pulling hers. My uncle and dad came running down the street to break the fight up because they saw me beating her ass. They told me to go to the house, and when I got there Stacey gave me a hug and said, "Thank you, little sister, for having my back." I said, "Anytime, big sister. I got your back."

Chapter 8

The Burning Bed

Stepmom had started to change. It became a nightmare with her seemingly overnight.

My dad was now working at a group home for kids. He used to be a Philadelphia police officer, but he retired when he got shot in the elbow while off-duty trying to protect and serve. I don't remember much of the details; I was very young at that time. But this new job required dad to spend several nights at work, and we wouldn't be able to see him for days. I would sometimes think that Dad cared more for the kids at the group home than he did for us. He never knew what was going on at home.

My dad drank so much that sometimes he'd fall asleep outside on the porch or in that ugly van of his. I hated when my dad and stepmom would drink. Their arguments weren't normal arguments; the way they

23

would argue, you would think someone was going to be murdered that night.

They went out one night to the neighborhood corner bar to have a few drinks when this lady walked up to my dad and started flirting with him. This lady didn't know that my dad was with anyone, and she was all over him while Stepmom was in the bathroom. He didn't mind it, because Dad was a major flirt himself. When Stepmom came back from the ladies' room, she walked up on them and said, "Who's this ugly whore, one of your side bitches?" He replied, "No, I don't even know this fucking lady, Glenda!" Mom stormed out of the bar and Dad went chasing after her.

Later that night, we were all in the bed asleep when I heard a lot of arguing going on in their bedroom. She was accusing him of cheating, and he was accusing her of being a crazy, sick drunk. If you ask me, they were both crazy, sick drunks—but nobody asked me, so I guess I'll just mind my business. I woke up from all the noise as they were throwing things and fighting each other. I didn't want to wake my sisters, so I just kept quiet and listened to them arguing and fighting.

Next thing you know, it got quiet for about a good five minutes. No sooner than I began to lay my head down and fall asleep, my dad came screaming and dashing out of the bedroom like a bat out of hell. He was trying to make his way to the bathroom with a ball of flames consuming his entire body. Yes, that crazy bitch stepmother of mine poured some gasoline on him and threw a match on the bed while he was asleep! She had tried to set him on fire. He ran to the shower, jumped in it, and washed the flames off him. I thought I was having a nightmare, but I noticed I was wide awake. All this time, I still didn't want to wake my sisters. I was too petrified to do anything at that moment.

Someone must have heard all the noise and called the police. When they arrived at our home, they asked Mom if everything was okay, and she told them that everything was fine. The officer then looked at my dad and asked him the same question. My dad just nodded his head and said, "Yes, sir, everything is fine." The police officer then left and told them to have a good night.

When the officer left, Stepmom drove Dad to the emergency room. They must have bandaged him up, because when they got back home, I saw he had white strips wrapped around his whole stomach and back area. They acted as if nothing happened and went to sleep. I finally dozed off after fighting to go to sleep. The next day came, and Stacey asked me if I saw what had happened. I told her yes, and we made a promise to each other not to say a word to anyone about what we saw.

Chapter 9

Busted Forehead

D ad and Stepmom didn't argue as much after that, and as a family we went on a lot of trips and traveled. Then, out of nowhere one day they had some great news: They were having a baby girl! *Oh, wow, another girl to take up space in this small three-bedroom home*, I thought. It was bad enough that I had to share the room with Stacey and Destiny—now there would be another sister.

When Shyra was born in January 1980, it was not the year for my sisters and me. We really got run around like we were the slaves of the house. Mom was so fucking lazy when it came to getting things for Shyra that I was really the one who always had to get the Pampers, bottles, something for her to drink, and whatever else her lazy ass came up with.

Stepmom didn't care too much for dark-skinned people. She's light-skinned, and she hated the fact that Destiny and I were dark. My nickname was Inky.

Stepmom would make fun of me by yelling, "Come here, Inky, with your black ass!" She would always say things like, "Your mom is black and ugly and so are you. Your mother didn't want you, and I can't stand you." In the back of my mind, I would be like, "That's why you a fat bitch." I knew if I said that out loud, though, she would slaughter me like a black pig.

Stacey and I were teenagers at the time. I was thirteen, Stacey was <u>fifteen, and</u> Destiny was eight years old. It's not like we were still young and didn't know what the fuck was going on.

I was outside on the porch with my friends one summer evening and Stepmom yelled for me to come in the house. She wanted me to go upstairs and get Shyra a diaper. I guess I wasn't moving fast enough, because as I walked in the house, she slapped the shit out of me. I mean, I saw stars, and the little Lucky Charms man was on them. When she slapped me, I busted my head on the padlock on the door. Blood started to trickle down from my forehead. I was so afraid because I didn't know what she would do next. She yelled, "See what you made me do! Get your black ass upstairs and wipe that blood off your face before your dad gets home, you dumb

28

bitch!" I ran upstairs to clean my face. When I came back downstairs, she told me to go into the kitchen, get a butter knife from the drawer, and press it on my forehead under the cut. She told me it would help the swelling go down before my dad got home. At that moment I wanted to fuck her up good; she didn't want Dad to see what she had done to me. I was hoping the knot on my forehead wouldn't go down so he could see what she did to me, hoping he would beat her ass.

Dad arrived home a few hours late. When he got in the house, he noticed I had a big knot on my forehead and asked me what happened. As if he couldn't see for his damn self. I tried to tell him, but she cut me off and told him that I made a mistake and bumped into the lock when I came in the door. I'm looking at her like, "You lying ass." I wanted to stab the shit out of her face, but all I could do was shake my head and take my ass upstairs to my room. She got away with another murder once again.

Lenita J Washington

Chapter 10

Stealing Food Out of the Plate

Stepmom always made sure our clothes were nice and clean and our hair was done. But when it came to making meals for us, she would give Mark and Stephan more food than Stacey, Destiny, and me. I mean, she fed us like baby birds and fed them like grizzly bears! They were growing, but still, that wasn't fair to us. So, I would take it upon myself to get more food.

As soon as we set the table to eat, I would take my fork and stick it in Mark's and Stephan's plates and take some of their food. They would say, "Hey, why you always taking our food?" I said, "Because you're too fat, and you don't need all of that food, so share." My sisters would just sit at the table and laugh at me. I told them that they better not tell.

She always gave us just a little bit. We could only have one serving, and we would still be hungry. That's one reason why my sisters and I could never gain weight;

we were so skinny. We had no choice, because she barely fed us! Her fat ass would make herself a big plate and then get second servings. She was just plain old mean.

Chapter 11

Going Away to Camp

It was early July, and of course that meant it was summer vacation for us. We all were shipped away for summer camp up in the mountains except for Destiny and Shyra, because they were too young. I couldn't wait to go and stay there for the four-week getaway. But I was also afraid and sad for my sister when we left. Stacey and I cried our little eyes out when it were time to board the bus. We stared out the bus windows, crying and waving bye to our little sister.

We arrived at camp and got to take part in so many activities. We went swimming and enjoyed recreational arts and crafts, theatre classes, drawing contests, and bonfires. We even wrote letters and made a few calls back home. I was deeply satisfied to know that Destiny was okay, so that made my vacation at camp even better.

Soon the four weeks were up, and it was time to go back home to the hell house. Stacey and I weren't ready to go back to that place. Maybe Mark and Stephan were, because the camp staff fed us like we were in prison. You know their fat asses weren't having that; they liked to eat! I think they had probably lost a few pounds while they were there. Shit . . . hell, they needed to. But now they were about to put those pounds back on, because were on our way back home.

Chapter 12

The Broken Arm

Stacey and I were now in middle school making new friends. I was still running track and doing my after-school activities. For the most part, everything seemed great, and Stepmom and Dad weren't fighting anymore. I thought things were looking up until one day, Stacey pissed off Stepmom.

Stepmom asked Stacey to go to the corner store to pick up some items for the house. After paying for everything, Stacey took a quarter out of the change to buy herself a peppermint patty. When she got home from the store, Stepmom noticed twenty-five cents was missing from the change. She asked, "Stacey, did you take twenty-five cents from my change?" and she replied, "Yes, ma'am." See, if that was me, I know I would had said, "Hell no!" I would have taken that lie straight to my grave! She was going to whip your ass whether you were telling the truth or not, so I'd rather just lie.

Stepmom said, "Stacey, get me a shoe. Go to my room so I can whip your ass." Stacey started crying, saying, "No, Mommy, I won't steal anymore! I'm sorry, please don't beat me!" I was in our bedroom with Destiny, holding each other and crying for our sister. Stepmom closed her bedroom door and started beating Stacey. All I could hear was Stacey screaming and a loud thumping coming from the room. After getting a beating, Stacey came into the room with us. She still was crying. We gave her a hug and I noticed her arm was swollen and bruised. Stacey was in a lot of pain, and her arm looked bad.

The next day on our way to school, Stacey was complaining to me about her arm hurting. When she got to class, the teacher noticed something disturbing about Stacey's arm and sent her to the nurse's office. The nurse took a look at her arm and was surprised at what she had seen. She asked, "What in the world happened to your arm, my dear?" Stacey said, "I fell on the rocks on the way to school this morning." She didn't believe that, of course. The nurse said, "Well . . . you know you fractured your arm badly?" Stacey said, "Yes, ma'am," and just looked away and put her head down. The nurse wrapped her arm up, called our parents, and Dad was on his way.

Daddy came to pick Stacey up from school and took her to the emergency room. The doctor examined her arm and told Dad he would have to put a cast on her arm. Daddy said okay, then turned to Stacey and asked her with frustration in his voice, "Stacey, what happened to your arm?" She told him the same story she told the nurse. Dad told her to be careful, kissed her on the forehead, and gave her a hug.

When they got home from the hospital, everyone was already home from school and Stepmom was still at work. It was cool that Stacey had a cast on her arm, because everybody wanted to sign their name on it. I asked, "Why didn't you tell the truth about Stepmom beating you with a shoe?" She said, "I just wanted Daddy to pick me up from school. I just wanted Daddy!"

There were many days we wanted our dad to save us from Stepmom but telling him the truth about the abuse just wasn't worth it to us. We felt like no one would listen or believe us anyway. So, it was better for us to keep quiet, keep our heads down, and pretend like everything was alright, because telling the truth would only make our situation worse.

Chapter 13

Doing Homework

I enjoyed going to school. Every week I couldn't wait for the weekend to be over so I could go back to school Monday through Friday. It was like my getaway vacation from being with my evil stepmother. I would think about how my sisters, and I were like Cinderella, and Ms. Glenda was our evil stepmother.

On my way home from school, I would start to get depressed. I knew once I walked through that door it was all over for me. Stepmom didn't care for me or Destiny because our complexion was dark; she despised anyone with dark skin. Her own son Mark was dark-skinned, but he got a pass because that was her biological son. Stacey, my oldest sister, was light-skinned, so she didn't get beaten as much.

We all had to be at the table doing our homework before Stepmother got home from work. I hated math. It just wasn't one of my strong points in school; science was. Before we could go outside, Stepmother would check our homework. Here I went once again, always finishing up my homework last.

When Stepmom checked my homework one day, I had a few math problems wrong. She would go over the math problems with me, but it felt like everlasting torture. This particular day, I was really having a hard time with a few questions. She started yelling at me, "What is the answer to this math problem?!" I was crying, nervous, and shaking, hoping I would get it right. I think I was having an anxiety attack. Scared to say the wrong answer, because I knew I didn't have the answer, I told her, "I don't know the answer. I think it's four?"

Then she got close to my face, dug her finger into my cheek, and screamed in my ear, "You do know the answer, DUMBASS! What's the answer?!" She was screaming so loud that the spit from her mouth landed on my face. I was thinking if I didn't get this answer right, I was as good as dead, so I started praying I'd get it right. I replied again, "I don't know the answer." Lord, why did I say that? The next thing I knew, she slapped me in the face with an open hand followed up with a closed fist and punched me right in my nose, which knocked me on the floor. As I got up, my nose was bleeding and she yelled, "Get your dumb ass up and get some tissue for your nose!!" As I walked away to get some tissue, she began to chastise me. "You're a black, inky, dumb whore. Your mother is a whore, and you'll be a whore, too, with your dumb black ass!!"

After I came back from cleaning up the blood from my nose, she called me some more names, knocked me around a few more times, and I finally got the answer right. After that ordeal, I decided I didn't want to go outside anymore. I was pretty banged up from crying, being slapped, and punched in the face by Stepmom.

Later that evening, my step-brothers and sisters all came in the house from playing outside and went to go wash their hands for dinner. Everybody just stared at me while we were having dinner because my face was red and swollen. I just sat there with my head down, crying and eating my food, because if Stepmother had seen me crying, I would have been given another beat down. Normally I would take food out of Mark and Stephan's plates, but that night I didn't have the energy to do so.

Chapter 14

Tissue Left on the Toilet Seat

It was summertime, and that's when we would take family vacations. We had some great family moments on our trips. We would visit Sesame Place, Crystal Cave, and Georgia for our family reunion.

When we came back from one of our family outings, Dad went out to drink with his buddies like he usually did. Stepmom would stay in the house and have a few drinks by herself.

One day while just Stepmom was at home I had to go to the bathroom and do the number two. We weren't allowed to say the word "dookie" in our house; if you did, you would get slapped in the back of your head. So, I guess I learned something through the abuse.

I would put tissue around the toilet seat so my butt wouldn't get wet from the piss left on the seat. Mark and Stephan would urinate on the toilet seat and that was so annoying to me, so I found a way around it.

As I finished up, I flushed the toilet and went downstairs. Ten minutes later, I remembered I had left the tissue on the toilet seat, and it was a lot.

Stepmother happened to go into the bathroom at that same time and noticed all the tissue lined up around the toilet seat. Oh my—I knew it was about to be trouble, trouble, trouble. She screamed downstairs, "Who put all this tissue on this toilet seat?!" Mark, Stephan, Stacy, Destiny, and I looked at each other with the *"oh, shit" look*. No one answered, so she came downstairs and asked again, "Who put all that damn tissue on the toilet seat?!"

We all said, "Not *me*," at different times. She looked at me and Destiny and said, "Did one of your black asses do it?!" We both replied, "No, Mommy." Stepmother said, "I don't believe neither one of you! Get your black asses in the dining room so I can beat your ass!!" Stepmother went to go get an extension cord, and my siblings started cleaning up the house. That's what we would always do when someone was about to get a whooping or get in some type of trouble. We didn't want to be the next target, so we would start cleaning up.

Stepmother pushed the dining room table back toward the wall and pulled the chair out. She told Destiny to pull her pants and panties down and lay across the chair. She took the extension cord high in the air and whacked Destiny across her butt real hard. Destiny started screaming and crying, saying, "Stop, Mommy, I didn't do it!!" I was standing on the side, watching and crying because I knew I was next, and I was the one that did it, but I knew if I told on myself that it would only make my beating worse.

She continued to beat Destiny, then she told me to pull my panties down as well. She gave me my first whack across my butt, and it felt like my skin was being ripped from my soul. I screamed, "Mommy, stop, please, I don't want any more!!" She continued to beat us back and forth for five minutes or so, which seemed like forever. Stepmother decided to stop beating me and told me to put my clothes back on, go upstairs, and stay in my room. Unfortunately, Destiny continued to receive whacks across her butt. After she got finished whipping Destiny, she sent her upstairs to stay in the room as well.

She put us both on punishment, and when Destiny came in the room, she was crying and bleeding from her butt. When I saw the blood seeping through her white panties, I began to cry more and felt bad because it was all my fault. I could have told the truth and saved her, but I didn't; I was being selfish. She couldn't sit on the bed because her butt was bleeding and in so much pain. My butt wasn't bleeding; however, it was in a great deal of pain. I reached over, gave Destiny a hug, and whispered in her ear, "I'm sorry, sister."

Chapter 15

Tried To Drown Me In The Kitchen Sink

A few weeks later, once our butts recovered and we were off punishment, we were able to go outside and play with our friends, and just in time to join the block party we had in our neighborhood.

All the grills were going and there was great music, games, and lots of fun. My favorite foods to eat were the burgers and crabs. I would work my way from the beginning to the end of the block, collecting food for my plate. Everybody else was jumping rope, playing jacks, playing wall ball, or just being up to no good. Me, I stayed eating—that was good enough for me.

Next thing I knew, I heard Stepmother calling my name. I tried to ignore it; however, my friends were teasing me, saying, "Your mother's calling you." I rolled my eyes at them, threw my plate in the trash, and ran down to the house to see what she wanted. She always calling me to help her with Shyra. I was like, I have four other siblings—why can't she bother them? Stacey was right there; she never left the porch.

I got to the house and before I could even say, "Yes, Mommy?" she slapped me in my face as soon as I walked in the door. I grabbed my face and started crying, saying, "I'm sorry, what did I do, Mommy?" She said, "Get your fucking ass in here, you're moving too slow!!" She then grabbed me by my neck and flung me from the living room all the way into the kitchen. I still didn't understand—what in the heck did I do wrong? I had just been outside eating my food, minding my own business.

When we got in the kitchen, she jerked my neck some more and yelled, "Oh, you think you're cute, with that baby hair around your edges?" I was crying with my head down, saying, "No, Mommy, I don't think I'm cute." She yelled, "Yes you do!!"and began to snatch my baby hairs from my edges. I started screaming and crying, trying to break away. I couldn't get away because she had a tight grip around my neck. I was hoping somebody would walk in the house so she would stop, but no one never did.

She then began to drag me toward the sink by my hair and neck. I noticed that there was a sink full of water with nothing in it. She dunked my face into the water, holding my neck and head down, fully submerged in the water. As she attempted to drown me, she pulled my face from out of the water and said, "So you think you're cute, but you're not! You're fucking ugly!!" then dunked my face back into the water. I kept fighting to get her hands off my head, but I couldn't breathe, and water was splashing everywhere. It was a torture situation that I just couldn't get myself out of. She repeatedly dunked my head in and out of the water and called me ugly all the while. After a while, I suppose she was exhausted, because she finally stopped.

When she was finished trying to drown me in the kitchen sink, she smacked me one last time in the face and said, "Now take your ugly black ass outside." I replied, crying, "I can't go back outside looking like this! My hair is messed up now." She replied, "I don't care, Ladesa, go outside just like that!!" I went outside as I was told, looking like I had been in a freaking cat fight. All my neighborhood friends started pointing and clowning me as I sat down on my porch steps. I wasn't in the mood to play anymore; I just felt hurt, ugly, and humiliated. As I cried, Stacey and Destiny sat down next to me and began to hug me and wipe my tears from my face while Stepmother stood in the doorway looking at us with disgust on her face.

Chapter 16

Fighting Over Destiny

The next day we went to Sunday morning church. We had to be there early because all of us were in the choir and I had to practice for my solo part. Stepmom had us in church on Sunday, Wednesday for Bible study, and Saturday for choir rehearsal. We stayed in church all the time. You would think since we were a churchgoing family, Stepmother wouldn't have been such a mean, evil stepmother.

After church service was over, all the members would go down into the basement of the church and have Sunday dinner, as they called it. We had fried chicken, collard greens, mac and cheese, cornbread, ham, and mashed potatoes. You name it, we had it all! This was the moment we would all come together, eat, laugh, and love one another.

Once church dinner was over, we headed home to take off our Sunday wear. I couldn't wait to get home to get out of those itchy pantyhose.

Stacey and I started picking out clothes to wear to school for the next day. Destiny would laugh and throw our clothes at us while were trying them on. Then we would start playing dress-up, putting our clothes on Destiny. She'd say, "Sisters, can you put that outfit on me? I want to wear that!" Then I'd do her hair, and once she had the outfit on and her hair was all done up, Destiny would walk down the hallway with her hands on her hips like she was a model. Stacey and I would chant and cheer her on by saying, "Go Destiny, go Destiny!!"

Stacey told us to be quiet for a minute because she was listening to Stepmom's conversation on the phone. She said, "I think you're about to leave us, Destiny." Destiny giggled and said, "No, I'm not." I said, "Why you say that Stacey? Stop playing." She replied, "No, seriously, I heard Stepmom say, 'We'll drop off Destiny soon." We stopped playing dress-up, got really quiet, and tears began to run down our faces.

Stepmom came upstairs into the room where we were playing and told Destiny to get dressed and pack up all her clothes, because she was going back home to our real mother for good. My sisters and I started crying and my Stepmom yelled, "Oh, stop crying and help her pack her shit, and hurry!!" We packed all her bags while Dad and Stepmom waited downstairs. We walked Destiny downstairs, and all of us hugged her before she left. Stacey and I ran to the window to see Destiny pull off and began to cry and waved goodbye.

Later that day, Dad and Stepmom returned from dropping off Destiny, and the house just seemed empty to me knowing that our younger sister Destiny wasn't with us anymore. Stacey and I were sad and broken, Stephan and Mark just went on with their regular play fighting around the house, and Shyra was too young to understand much of anything that was going on.

We had a late dinner that day, and while sitting at the table a call came through. It was my real mom, and she had called to tell my dad to come back and pick up Destiny. All you could hear was my mother yelling on the other end, saying, "Come back and pick her ass up, right now!" My dad said, "For what, Janelle? You wanted her, and now you got her!" Stacey and I glanced at each other with smiles on our faces, like *YES!* Then, next thing you know Stepmom opened her big mouth in the background and said, "No, we are not going to pick her up. She can keep her!" I was like, *Oh, for crying out loud, shut the hell up,* in the back of my head. So, Dad and Stepmom went back and forth about the situation while were eating and finally hung up the phone up with my mom.

After eating dinner, my brothers, sisters, and I went in our rooms to play while Dad and Stepmom were downstairs having a few adult drinks, discussing if they should pick Destiny up or not. My mom kept ringing the house phone profusely because she wanted a definitive answer. I was like, *This thing is about to go down,* because when Dad and Stepmom be drinking their liquor . . . *oh boy, it's on and popping!*

After a few drinks and hours later, Dad and Stepmom came into our rooms and told us to get up and put our clothes on. I'm looking at them like, *What in the hell! Oh, my goodness, here they go with the drunk shit.* So, we dragged ourselves out of the bed, put our clothes on, and waited on the couch for them to tell us our next move. You can imagine how sleepy we looked because of how late it was.

Dad and Stepmom came stumbling down the steps, yelling at us, "Wake up, come on, and get in the van! We're going to get your sister!" We all jumped up off the couch and shouted, "Yay!" but in the back of my mind I was like, *I hope we can make it with these two drunk asses.*

So, we finally pulled up in front of my mom's house in Willow Grove. She was living with my older cousins and some other unknown folks. My dad beeped the horn, but no one came outside. After waiting awhile, Dad decided to knock at the door and some unfamiliar person answered the door. Dad told the person that he was here to pick up his daughter, but all you could hear in the background was my mother yelling from another room, "You can't have her, close the door!" Next thing you know, my Stepmom, having heard all the ruckus going on, jumped out of the car, ran up to the door, and kicked the door open, screaming, "Give her to us!"

We were left in the car by ourselves, scared and afraid of what might be happening inside the house. All we heard coming from the house was screaming, fighting, and things being thrown and broken. I was hoping the cops would come, but they never did. It was like they were in there fighting forever until I finally saw Destiny come out the door by herself with her nightgown on and no shoes. My sisters, brothers, and I were in the car yelling out the windows, "Run, Destiny, run!" Destiny started to run, and then the next thing we knew my dad and stepmom were running out of the house as well. My mom, and whoever she was with, tried to chase after them, but they stopped and started to throw rocks at them and the vehicle we were in. Dad scooped up Destiny as he was running towards the vehicle, they jumped in the van, and we pulled off.

Blood was dripping down their faces, and Stepmom's hair was looking wild and crazy like she had been in a catfight and lost. We were so happy to have Destiny back that we forgot all about the fighting they had done to get her back. We all just stated singing, "We are family, I got all my sisters with me!" and hugged each other, crying for joy.

* 9 7 9 8 9 8 5 6 2 5 3 0 1 *